WHAT IS THE BOOK OF PHILIPPIANS?

Kids' Guides to God's Word Series

What Is the Book of Genesis?
What Is the Book of Exodus?
What Is the Book of Leviticus?
What Is the Book of Numbers?
What Is the Book of Deuteronomy?
What Is the Book of Joshua?
What Is the Book of Judges?
What Is the Book of Ruth?
What Is the Book of 1 Samuel?
What Is the Book of 2 Samuel?
What Is the Book of 1 Kings?
What Is the Book of 2 Kings?
What Are the Books of 1–2 Chronicles?
What Are the Books of Ezra & Nehemiah?
What Is the Book of Esther?
What Is the Book of Job?
What Is the Book of Psalms?
What Is the Book of Proverbs?
What Is the Book of Ecclesiastes?
What Are the Books of Song of Songs & Lamentations?
What Is the Book of Isaiah?
What Is the Book of Jeremiah?
What Is the Book of Ezekiel?
What Is the Book of Daniel?
What Are the Books of Hosea–Micah?
What Are the Books of Nahum–Malachi?

What Is the Gospel of Matthew?
What Is the Gospel of Mark?
What Is the Gospel of Luke?
What Is the Gospel of John?
What Is the Book of Acts?
What Is the Book of Romans?
What Is the Book of 1 Corinthians?
What Is the Book of 2 Corinthians?
What Is the Book of Galatians?
What Is the Book of Ephesians?
What Is the Book of Philippians?
What Are the Books of Colossians & Philemon?
What Are the Books of 1–2 Thessalonians?
What Are the Books of 1–2 Timothy & Titus?
What Is the Book of Hebrews?
What Is the Book of James?
What Are the Books of 1–2 Peter & Jude?
What Are the Books of 1-3 John?
What Is the Book of Revelation?

What Is the Book of

PHILIPPIANS?

Michael Whitworth

ISBN 978-1-971767-33-8

Published by Start2Finish
Bend, Oregon 97702
start2finish.org

Printed in the United States of America

30 29 28 27 26 1 2 3 4 5

CONTENTS

INTRODUCTION

Have you ever gotten a letter or a message from someone you love at exactly the moment you needed it most? Maybe you were having the worst week of your life, and your phone buzzed with a text from a friend who said exactly the right thing. Maybe you found a note in your lunchbox on a day when school felt impossible. Maybe someone far away sent you something that reminded you they hadn't forgotten you, that you weren't alone, that things were going to be okay.

Now imagine getting a letter like that from a man sitting in a Roman prison, chained to a soldier, waiting for a trial that could end with his execution. And imagine that the letter isn't full of complaints or fear or self-pity. Instead, it's full of *joy*. Deep, stubborn, unshakable joy. The kind of joy that doesn't make sense given the circumstances, the kind that can only come from someone who has found something more valuable than comfort, more durable than safety, more real than anything the world can offer.

That's the letter to the Philippians. And the man who wrote it was the apostle Paul.

WHY THIS LETTER MATTERS

Philippians is short. Only four chapters, 104 verses. You could read the whole thing in fifteen minutes. But packed into those four chapters is some of the most powerful, personal, and beloved writing in the entire New Testament.

This is where Paul writes, "To live is Christ and to die is gain." This is where he describes Jesus emptying himself and taking the form of a servant, humbling himself all the way to a cross, and being exalted by God above every name. This is where he tells us to "rejoice in the Lord always," to be anxious about nothing, to think about whatever is true and noble and right. This is where he reveals the secret of contentment and declares, "I can do all this through him who gives me strength."

If you've spent any time in church, you've probably heard some of those verses. But hearing them as isolated quotes is like hearing a few notes from a song without knowing the melody. Philippians was written as a single letter, meant to be read from beginning to end in one sitting. When you read it that way, the pieces come together into something extraordinary: a picture of what it looks like to live with Jesus at the center of absolutely everything.

HOW IT ALL STARTED

To understand Philippians, you need to know how Paul and this church found each other.

Around AD 49, Paul crossed the Aegean Sea from Asia into Europe for the first time. He landed in the region of Macedonia, in northern Greece, and made his way to a city called Philippi. It was a Roman colony, a place fiercely proud of its connection to Rome. Many of its residents were retired soldiers or their descendants, and the city operated almost like a miniature Rome, complete with Roman laws, Roman customs, and Roman citizenship.

Paul didn't find a synagogue in Philippi. There may not have been enough Jewish residents to form one. Instead, he found a small group of women gathered by a river for prayer. One of them was a businesswoman named Lydia, who sold expensive purple cloth. God opened her heart to respond to Paul's message, and she and her entire household were baptized. She immediately invited Paul and his companions to stay at her home.

Things escalated quickly. Paul cast a spirit out of a slave girl who had been making money for her owners through fortune-telling. The owners were furious. They dragged Paul and his companion Silas before the authorities, who had them stripped, beaten, and thrown into prison. At midnight, while Paul and Silas were singing hymns in their cell, an earthquake shook the prison open. The jailer, terrified, was about to kill himself when Paul stopped him. That night, the jailer and his whole family believed the gospel and were baptized.

So the church at Philippi was born out of a prayer meeting by a river, a businesswoman's open heart, a slave girl's liberation, a wrongful imprisonment, a midnight earthquake, and a jailer's conversion. From the very beginning, this church was marked by unlikely people, dramatic circumstances, and the unmistakable hand of God.

Over the next decade, the Philippians became Paul's closest partners. They supported him financially when no other church did. They sent him money in Thessalonica. They contributed to his work across the region. And when they heard Paul was in prison again, this time in Rome, they sent one of their own, a man named Epaphroditus, carrying a gift and their love.

Paul wrote this letter in return. It's a thank-you note, a progress report, a heartfelt plea for unity, and a love letter all wrapped into one.

WHAT YOU'RE ABOUT TO READ

Here's where we're headed in the chapters ahead:

Paul opens by thanking God for the Philippians and praying that their love will keep growing. He reports on his imprisonment and reveals that, far from silencing the gospel, his chains have actually advanced it. He wrestles honestly with the possibility of death, and gives us the stunning declaration that for him, living means Christ and dying means profit.

Then he turns to the Philippians' own situation. He urges them to stand together, to put others first, and to stop the grumbling that threatens their unity. To show them what humility really looks like, he points them to Jesus, who gave up the glory of heaven to become a servant, who went all the way to a criminal's death on a cross, and who was then exalted by God above everything that exists.

He holds up two real-life examples of that same selfless spirit, Timothy and Epaphroditus, and then tells his own story: how he traded the most impressive religious résumé imaginable for the surpassing worth of knowing Christ. He warns against people who would pull the Philippians backward into empty religion, and he casts a vision for the future that makes every present hardship look small: a day when Christ will return and transform everything.

The letter closes with practical instructions on joy, peace, contentment, and generosity, and with one of the warmest expressions of gratitude in all of Paul's writing.

WHY THIS MATTERS FOR YOU

You don't have to be in a Roman prison to need this letter. You just have to be alive in a world that constantly tells you your worth depends on what you achieve, what you own, and what people think of you. You just have to be someone who gets anxious, who struggles with comparison, who wonders if God is really enough when everything else feels uncertain.

Philippians speaks into all of that. It says there is a joy deeper than your circumstances. It says there is a peace that doesn't require understanding. It says that the God who started something in you will finish it. And it says that the secret to life isn't getting more but knowing Christ.

BEFORE YOU BEGIN

A few things to keep in mind as you read.

This is a letter, not a story. Unlike Genesis or Joshua or 1 Samuel, Philippians doesn't follow a narrative from beginning to end. It's a real letter written by a real person to real people about real problems. That means it jumps between topics the way letters do. Paul moves from thanksgiving to autobiography to theology to practical instructions, sometimes within a few sentences. Don't worry if it feels different from the Old Testament books. Letters have their own rhythm, and once you find it, Paul's voice is one of the warmest and most compelling in all of Scripture.

The joy is not naïve. When Paul tells the Philippians to rejoice, he isn't pretending everything is fine. He's in chains. People are preaching Christ to spite him. His friends are suffering. He might die. Paul's joy isn't the shallow happiness that depends on things going well. It's a deep, hard-won conviction that Christ is worth more than anything he could lose. That kind of joy doesn't ignore pain. It looks pain in the face and keeps singing.

Everything points to Jesus. The letter begins and ends "in Christ Jesus." The centerpiece is a hymn about Christ's descent from heaven to a cross and his exaltation above every name. Paul's autobiography is about knowing Christ. His instructions are about living like Christ. His hope is about being with Christ. If you want to understand what it means for one person to be completely captivated by Jesus, read Philippians.

This is a short letter. But it has changed lives for two thousand years. It was written by a man in chains who was freer than anyone reading it. And the Christ it points to is the same yesterday, today, and forever.

Turn the page.

1

PARTNERS IN THE GOSPEL

Have you ever watched the movie *Cool Runnings*? It's based on the true story of Jamaica's first bobsled team. Four athletes from a tropical island decide to compete in the Winter Olympics, a sport they've never tried, in a place colder than anything they've ever experienced. Everyone laughs at them. Nobody thinks they belong. And the coach they recruit, a former bobsled champion named Irv Blitzer, is a disgraced athlete who hasn't coached anyone in years.

But here's the thing. Something real develops between that coach and those athletes. Irv doesn't just train them; he believes in them when nobody else does. And they don't just follow his instructions; they trust him with everything they have. Irv writes their training plans, cheers from the sidelines, and fights for them behind the scenes. Even when things go wrong, even when the bobsled crashes at the Olympics and their chance at finishing slips away, the bond between them holds. They carry the sled across the finish line together, and the whole stadium rises to its feet.

That kind of bond—built through shared struggle, fueled by genuine love, held together by something deeper than success—is exactly what we find at the very beginning of Paul's letter to the Philippians.

Paul isn't writing from a comfortable office. He's writing from a Roman prison. And he isn't writing to strangers. He's writing to people who have stood with him through thick and thin, who sent him money when he was broke, who sent a friend to care for him when he was locked up, who kept believing in the gospel when it cost them dearly. And even though Paul is chained up and far away, his letter practically glows with joy, gratitude, and confidence.

Let's see why.

A LETTER FROM A SERVANT

Paul opens his letter the way most people in the ancient world did: by saying who he is, who he's writing to, and giving a greeting. But Paul isn't ordinary, and he doesn't settle for an ordinary opening. Every word is loaded.

"Paul and Timothy, servants of Christ Jesus, to all God's holy people in Christ Jesus at Philippi, together with the overseers and deacons: Grace and peace to you from God our Father and the Lord Jesus Christ."

The first word Paul uses to describe himself is interesting: *servants*. The word he chose was even stronger than that. It meant "slaves." Not hired help. Not assistants. Slaves. People who belonged completely to someone else.

Now, slavery was common in the Roman world. Paul's readers knew exactly what a slave was. A slave didn't set his own schedule. He didn't pick his own assignments. His life belonged entirely to his master.

But there was another layer. In the Old Testament, some of the greatest heroes were called "servants of the Lord." Moses was God's servant. Joshua was God's servant. David was God's servant. It was a title of honor, given to people who lived their entire lives under God's authority and for God's mission.

Paul is saying both things at once. He and Timothy belong to Jesus completely. They live for him. They serve at his command. And there's no higher honor than that.

Notice what Paul does *not* call himself here. In many of his other letters, Paul introduces himself as an apostle, someone specially chosen and sent by Jesus. But he doesn't do that with the Philippians. He doesn't need to remind them of his authority. The relationship between them is so strong, so full of trust, that he can skip the title and simply say: I'm a servant of Jesus, just like you.

ALL GOD'S HOLY PEOPLE

Paul addresses the letter to "all God's holy people in Christ Jesus at Philippi." Other translations say "saints." When you hear the word "saint," you might picture someone in a stained-glass window, hands folded, halo glowing. But that's not what Paul means at all.

In the Bible, "holy people" or "saints" simply means people who have been set apart by God. Way back in the book of Exodus, God told the Israelites, "You will be for me a kingdom of priests and a holy nation" (Exodus 19:6). They were holy not because they were perfect but because God had claimed them as his own. Paul is saying the same thing about the Philippian Christians. God has called them out of their old lives and made them his people.

And notice that little word *all*. Paul says it over and over in this opening section: all God's people, all my prayers, all of you, all of you again. He mentions leaders by name, "overseers and deacons," the people who guided and served the congregation. But his letter isn't just for the leaders. It's for everyone. Paul isn't picking sides or playing favorites. He's writing to the whole church, because what he has to say matters for every single person in it.

Paul also squeezes in a greeting that sounds simple but is packed with meaning: "Grace and peace to you from God our Father and the Lord Jesus Christ." In the ancient world, the standard greeting in a letter was basically "Hello" or "Best wishes." But Paul swaps out the common greeting and replaces it with something bigger. *Grace* is God's undeserved love poured out on people who could never earn it. *Peace* is the result of that love, the deep wholeness and rest that come from being right with God. Grace is what God gives. Peace is what we experience because of it. Both come "from God our Father and the Lord Jesus Christ," placed side by side as the source of everything good.

A PRAYER FULL OF JOY

With the greeting finished, Paul moves into something deeply personal. He tells the Philippians how he prays for them. And what he says next reveals a relationship that most churches would envy.

"I thank my God every time I remember you. In all my prayers for all of you, I always pray with joy because of your partnership in the gospel from the first day until now."

Think about that for a second. Paul is in prison. He could be bitter. He could be anxious. He could complain about the people who put him there or the churches that forgot about him. Instead, every time the Philippians cross his mind, he thanks God for them. And he doesn't just thank God quietly. He prays for them *with joy*. Joy is going to come up again and again in this letter. In fact, some form of the word "joy" or "rejoice" appears sixteen times in these four short chapters. That's remarkable for a man writing from a prison cell.

But what exactly is Paul so thankful for? Their "partnership in the gospel from the first day until now." Partnership is a big word in this letter. It means more than just agreeing with someone. It means rolling up your sleeves and doing the work together, sharing the load, putting your own resources on the line.

The Philippians had done exactly that. When Paul first came to Philippi around AD 49, a group of women gathered by the river to pray, and a businesswoman named Lydia became one of his first converts (Acts 16:14). Paul was beaten and thrown in jail in Philippi. An earthquake broke the prison doors open, and the jailer and his whole family came to faith (Acts 16:25-34). From that rocky beginning, a church was born. And that church never stopped supporting Paul.

When he moved on to other cities, they sent him money. When he was locked up in prison again, they sent a man named Epaphroditus to care for him. No other church supported Paul the way the Philippians did. They were true partners, invested with their time, their money, and their lives. And they had been doing it for more than ten years without quitting. "From the first day until now."

THE GOOD WORK GOD WILL FINISH

Paul's gratitude flows naturally into one of the most encouraging verses in the entire Bible: "Being confident of this, that he who began a good work in you will carry it on to completion until the day of Christ Jesus."

Read that again slowly. It's one of my favorite verses in the Bible. God started something in the Philippians. He brought them to faith. He planted his love in their hearts. He began transforming them from the inside out. And Paul is absolutely confident that God won't abandon that project halfway. He will carry it to completion.

This isn't confidence in the Philippians' willpower. Paul isn't saying, "I'm sure you guys will keep it together." He's saying, "I'm sure *God* will keep it together." The God who began the good work is the same God who will finish it. And the finish line isn't some vague hope. It's "the day of Christ Jesus," the day when Jesus returns and makes all things right, the day when every Christian will stand complete before him.

This matters because the Christian life can feel like an unfinished construction project. You start strong, you stumble, you wonder if you'll ever get it right. Paul wants the Philippians to know that their salvation isn't dependent on their ability to hold on. It depends on God's commitment to never let go.

A HEART ON DISPLAY

Paul's emotions pour out in the next verses. "It is right for me to feel this way about all of you, since I have you in my heart and, whether I am in chains or defending and confirming the gospel, all of you share in God's grace with me. God can testify how I long for all of you with the affection of Christ Jesus."

This is not religious small talk. Paul is bearing his heart. He tells them he carries them in his heart. Whether he's in chains or standing before a court to defend the gospel, they are with him. They share in God's grace together, partners in the same mission, bound by the same Lord.

Then Paul uses some of the strongest language in any of his letters. He says God himself can testify how much he longs for the Philippians "with the affection of Christ Jesus." That phrase means Paul doesn't just love them with his own human love. He loves them with the kind of tender, deep care that comes from Jesus himself. It's as if Christ's own love for this church flows through Paul like a river.

This is what genuine Christian community looks like. Not people who happen to attend the same building on Sundays. Not people who politely nod at each other in the hallway. Real partnership. Real love. Real sacrifice. People who share each other's burdens across distance and time and difficulty.

A PRAYER FOR WHAT MATTERS MOST

Paul doesn't just thank God for the Philippians. He also asks God for something specific on their behalf. And what he prays for tells us a lot about what matters most.

"And this is my prayer: that your love may abound more and more in knowledge and depth of insight, so that you may be able to discern what is best and may be pure and blameless for the day of Christ, filled with the fruit of righteousness that comes through Jesus Christ, to the glory and praise of God."

Paul prays, first and foremost, for their *love* to grow. Not just a warm feeling, but a love that increases "in knowledge and depth of insight." He wants them to love wisely. He wants their love to be paired with understanding, so they can see clearly, make good decisions, and tell the difference between what's merely fine and what truly matters.

That's an important distinction. Paul isn't asking them to be smart for the sake of being smart. He's asking that their love would be so shaped by truth and wisdom that they could identify the best path forward in any situation. In a world full of distractions and false teachings, knowing the difference between what's good and what's *best* is one of the most important skills a Christian can develop.

And where does this road lead? Paul says it leads to being "pure and blameless for the day of Christ, filled with the fruit of righteousness that comes through Jesus Christ." This is about character. Paul wants them to arrive at the end, on the day when Jesus returns, with lives that reflect who they belong to. Not perfect lives, but lives marked by the kind of goodness that only comes from being connected to Jesus.

And the final destination of it all? "To the glory and praise of God." Every prayer, every act of love, every wise decision, every step of growth in the Christian life has one ultimate destination: God getting the glory. That's the point of everything.

God started the work. God sustains the work. And God gets the credit when the work is finished.

WHAT THIS MEANS FOR US

First, real partnership means sacrifice, not just agreement. The Philippians didn't just believe the same things Paul believed. They gave their money, sent their people, and stood with him when it was expensive and inconvenient. Partnership in the gospel isn't a handshake. It's a commitment. If you want to be part of what God is doing in the world, it's going to cost you something: your time, your comfort, maybe your money. That's what partnership looks like.

Second, God finishes what he starts. If you've trusted in Jesus, God has begun a work in you. And he isn't going to walk away from the project. You might feel like a mess. You might feel like you've failed too many times. But your salvation doesn't depend on your ability to keep it together. It depends on God's faithfulness, and he has never once abandoned a project he started. He will carry it to completion.

Third, love without wisdom is incomplete. Paul doesn't just pray for the Philippians to love more. He prays for their love to grow "in knowledge and depth of insight." Love is not just a feeling; it's a skill that needs to be sharpened. The more you understand God's word and God's ways, the better you'll know how to love the people around you well. Loving wisely means sometimes telling someone a hard truth, sometimes stepping back, and always seeking what's genuinely best for others, not just what feels good in the moment.

Fourth, everything is for God's glory. Paul's prayer doesn't end with the Philippians being happy or healthy. It ends with "the glory and praise of God." That's the compass that should point every decision we make. The purpose of your life isn't to be comfortable or successful by the world's standards. It's to reflect God's goodness so clearly that the people around you can see who he is.

TALKING POINTS

1. **Paul calls himself a "servant" (or "slave") of Christ Jesus.** What does it mean to live as if your life completely belongs to someone else? How would seeing yourself as a servant of Jesus change the way you make everyday decisions?

2. **The Philippians didn't just agree with Paul's message; they partnered with him by sending money, encouragement, and people to help.** What does genuine partnership in the gospel look like in your own life? How can you move beyond just believing good things to actually doing something about them?

3. **Paul says he is "confident" that God will finish the good work he started in the Philippians.** Why do you think it's important that our confidence is in God's faithfulness and not our own strength? How does that change the way you handle failure or setbacks?

4. **Paul prays for the Philippians' love to grow "in knowledge and depth of insight."** Why do you think love needs wisdom to go along with it? Can you think of a time when someone tried to be loving but, because they didn't understand the situation, it didn't help?

5. **Paul wrote this entire section from prison, and yet it overflows with joy and gratitude.** What does it tell you about joy that Paul could experience it in such a painful situation? How is the kind of joy Paul describes different from just being happy because things are going well?

Paul has opened his heart. He's poured out his gratitude, his love, and his prayers for a church that has stood with him through everything. But he hasn't told them yet what's happening on his end. How is the imprisonment going? Is the gospel still advancing? Is Paul hopeful or afraid? He's about to answer all of that.

Turn the page.

2

TO LIVE IS CHRIST

Frederick Douglass was born into slavery in Maryland around 1818. He was separated from his mother as an infant, beaten by overseers, and treated as property. By every measure, his story should have ended in silence. Enslaved people weren't supposed to read. They weren't supposed to write. They certainly weren't supposed to speak in public about what they'd been through. The entire system was designed to keep them invisible and voiceless.

But Douglass learned to read in secret. He escaped to freedom. And then he did the thing nobody expected: he told his story. His book, *Narrative of the Life of Frederick Douglass*, published in 1845, became one of the most powerful documents in American history. The suffering that was supposed to destroy him became the very thing that gave his voice its power. People who never would have listened to an abstract argument against slavery couldn't ignore the firsthand account of a man who had lived it. The chains that were meant to silence him ended up giving him something to say that changed a nation.

That idea, that the worst circumstances can produce the greatest results, is exactly what Paul wants the Philippians to understand about his imprisonment. He's chained up in Rome, awaiting a trial that could end with his execution. From the outside, it looks like the gospel has hit a wall. But Paul sees something the rest of the world has missed. The wall has become a doorway.

CHAINS THAT COULDN'T HOLD THE GOSPEL

Paul opens this section with a phrase that was common in ancient letters between friends: "I want you to know." It's essentially saying, "Let me catch you up on what's been going on." The Philippians already knew Paul was in prison. They had sent Epaphroditus with a gift to help him. They were worried. They wanted to know: Is Paul okay? Is the mission falling apart?

Paul's answer must have stunned them.

"Now I want you to know, brothers and sisters, that what has happened to me has actually served to advance the gospel. As a result, it has become clear throughout the whole palace guard and to everyone else that I am in chains for Christ. And because of my chains, most of the brothers and sisters have been encouraged to speak the word of God more courageously and fearlessly."

Did you catch that? Paul doesn't start with his suffering. He doesn't talk about the cold cell or the heavy chains. The very first thing he reports is that the gospel is advancing. The word "advance" is a military term. It describes an army pushing forward, gaining ground. Paul is saying that his chains haven't stopped the gospel. They've actually pushed it into places it never would have reached otherwise.

How? Two ways.

First, the palace guard had heard the gospel. The "palace guard" was the emperor's elite security force, stationed in Rome. These were some of the most powerful soldiers in the empire. They guarded Paul in rotating shifts, typically four hours at a time. Think about that. A different set of soldiers, chained to Paul every few hours, forced to listen to whatever he had to say. Paul wasn't going to waste that opportunity. By the time he wrote this letter, the entire guard knew why he was locked up: he was "in chains for Christ."

The empire locked Paul up to silence him. Instead, they gave him a captive audience. Literally!

Second, other Christians in Rome had grown bolder. When they saw Paul suffering for the gospel without flinching, it lit a fire in them. Most of them started speaking about Jesus "more courageously and fearlessly" than they had before. Paul's courage under pressure was contagious. His chains didn't just fail to silence the gospel. They amplified it.

NOT EVERYONE HAD THE RIGHT MOTIVES

But here's where things get complicated. Paul reveals that not everyone preaching Christ in Rome was doing it for the right reasons.

"It is true that some preach Christ out of envy and rivalry, but others out of goodwill. The latter do so out of love, knowing that I am put here for the defense of the gospel. The former preach Christ out of selfish ambition, not sincerely, supposing that they can stir up trouble for me while I am in chains."

Two groups were preaching about Jesus. One group genuinely loved Paul. They understood that God had placed him in prison for a purpose, and they stepped up to fill the gap, spreading the gospel while Paul couldn't do it himself. They were loyal teammates, covering for a teammate who was injured.

The other group? Their motives were ugly. They preached Christ, but they did it "out of envy and rivalry." They wanted to build their own reputations while Paul was stuck in chains. They thought their success would twist the knife, making Paul feel worse about being locked up.

These weren't false teachers preaching a different message. They were preaching the real gospel. The *message* was right, but their *hearts* were wrong. They wanted to hurt Paul, not help the cause.

So how did Paul respond? With bitterness? Anger? A demand that they stop?

None of the above.

WHAT DOES IT MATTER?

Paul's response is one of the most remarkable things he ever wrote: "But what does it matter? The important thing is that in every way, whether from false motives or true, Christ is preached. And because of this I rejoice."

Read that again. People were literally using the gospel as a weapon against him, and Paul said, "So what? Christ is being preached. That's all I care about."

This is only possible for someone whose identity is completely wrapped up in Jesus, not in his own reputation. Paul didn't care who got the credit. He didn't care if people liked him. He didn't care if some preachers were trying to make him look bad. As long as Christ was being proclaimed, Paul was happy. His joy wasn't tied to his circumstances or his reputation. It was tied to one thing: the gospel moving forward.

And then Paul adds something even more surprising: "Yes, and I will continue to rejoice." He's not just making peace with a bad situation. He's genuinely, deeply joyful. From a prison cell. With enemies circling. Facing a trial that could kill him.

FACING THE TRIAL

Paul's joy didn't come from ignoring reality. He knew exactly what was ahead. A trial before the Roman authorities was coming, and the outcome was uncertain. He could be released, or he could be executed. But Paul wasn't anxious about it.

"I eagerly expect and hope that I will in no way be ashamed, but will have sufficient courage so that now as always Christ will be exalted in my body, whether by life or by death."

Paul's concern wasn't saving his own skin. His concern was that Christ would be "exalted in my body," meaning that whatever happened to him physically, life or death, it would make Jesus look great. Paul wanted his trial to be a spotlight, not on himself, but on Jesus.

He had good reason for this confidence. The Philippians were praying for him. And he trusted that God's Spirit would give him the boldness he needed when the moment came. Paul had faced hostile crowds, angry mobs, shipwrecks, and beatings. Every time, God had given him the courage to stand firm. He expected the same thing now.

But the question lingered: What if the verdict was death?

THE MOST FAMOUS LINE IN THE LETTER

Paul's answer to that question produced this famous verse in Philippians: "For to me, to live is Christ and to die is gain." Just a few words that summarize an entire life. "To live is Christ." Everything Paul did, every breath, every conversation, every letter, every step, was about Jesus. Christ wasn't one part of Paul's life. Christ *was* his life. His purpose, his passion, his reason for getting up in the morning.

"And to die is gain." For most people, death is the ultimate loss. But Paul saw it differently. If he died, he would finally, fully be with the one he had been living for all along. Death wasn't a punishment. It was a promotion. It was the finish line of a race he'd been running for decades.

This doesn't mean Paul had a death wish. It means his hope was so anchored in what lay beyond this world that death had lost its power to terrify him. He could face the trial with total peace, because both outcomes were wins. Released? He gets to keep serving Christ. Executed? He gets to be with Christ. Either way, Christ.

TORN BETWEEN TWO GOOD THINGS

Paul then does something deeply personal. He lets the Philippians see his inner struggle. "If I am to go on living in the body, this will mean fruitful labor for me. Yet what shall I choose? I do not know! I am torn between the two: I desire to depart and be with Christ, which is better by far; but it is more necessary for you that I remain in the body."

Paul is being brutally honest. If the choice were purely about him, he'd choose death in a heartbeat, because being with Christ is "better by far." That's an extraordinary statement from a man who had accomplished more for God than almost anyone in history. With all the churches he'd planted, all the people he'd baptized, all the letters he'd written, Paul's assessment was: the best thing that could happen to me is to leave this world and be with Jesus.

But Paul didn't live for himself. He lived for others. And the Philippians still needed him. They needed his teaching, his encouragement, and his example. They were facing their own struggles, their own opposition. Walking away now, even to be with Christ, would mean leaving them without the help they needed.

So Paul set aside his personal preference and leaned into what was best for the people he loved.

CONFIDENT OF THE OUTCOME

Paul resolves the tension with quiet confidence: "Convinced of this, I know that I will remain, and I will continue with all of you for your progress and joy in the faith, so that through my being with you again your boasting in Christ Jesus will abound on account of me."

Paul believed God was going to get him out of prison. Not because prison was too hard, and not because Paul deserved freedom. But because the Philippians needed him. Their "progress and joy in the faith" depended, at least in part, on his continued ministry among them.

Notice those two words again: *progress* and *joy*. Paul used the word "progress" back in verse 12 to describe the advance of the gospel. Now he uses it to describe what he wants for the Philippians themselves. He wants them to move forward in their faith, to grow, to mature. And he wants them to experience deep joy as they do it. Progress without joy is just grinding. Joy without progress is just treading water. Paul wants both for them.

And the ultimate result? That when Paul comes back to Philippi, their "boasting in Christ Jesus will abound." Not boasting in Paul. Not boasting in themselves. Boasting in Christ. Paul wanted every good thing that happened, including his release from prison, to point straight back to Jesus.

WHAT THIS MEANS FOR US

First, God works through circumstances that look like setbacks. Paul's imprisonment looked like the end of his ministry. Instead, it opened doors that freedom never could have. The palace guard heard the gospel. Other Christians found their courage. The message spread faster than ever. When life takes a turn you didn't expect, don't assume God has lost control. He may be advancing his purposes in ways you can't see yet.

Second, the gospel is bigger than any one person. Paul rejoiced when people preached Christ even with selfish motives. He cared more about the message than about who got credit for delivering it. That's a hard standard to live up to, but it's the right one. If something good is happening for God's kingdom, be glad about it, even if the people doing it aren't your favorite people or aren't doing it the way you would.

Third, having one clear purpose changes everything. Paul could face prison, rivals, and the threat of death with joy because his life had one focus: Christ. When you know what you're living for, you can handle almost anything. Most of the anxiety and frustration we feel comes from not knowing what really matters to us, or from caring too much about things that don't last. Paul had it figured out. "To live is Christ and to die is gain." When Jesus is the center, everything else falls into place.

Fourth, loving others sometimes means setting aside what you want. Paul wanted to be with Christ. That was his deepest personal desire. But he chose to keep serving because the Philippians needed him. Real love isn't about getting what you want. It's about asking, "What do the people around me need?" and being willing to give it, even when it costs you something.

TALKING POINTS

1. **Paul says his imprisonment "actually served to advance the gospel."** Can you think of a time when something that seemed bad turned out to serve a greater purpose? Why is it so hard to see God's hand in difficult circumstances while you're still in the middle of them?

2. **Some people were preaching Christ "out of envy and rivalry," and Paul still rejoiced.** How is it possible to be glad about a good outcome even when the people producing it have wrong motives? Are there limits to this principle?

3. **Paul wrote, "To live is Christ and to die is gain."** What would it look like for a person your age to honestly say, "To live is Christ"? What are some things that compete with Jesus for the center spot in our lives?

4. **Paul was "torn between" wanting to be with Christ and wanting to stay and serve the Philippians.** Have you

ever been torn between something you wanted for yourself and something someone else needed from you? How did you decide what to do?

5. **Paul's courage in prison inspired other Christians to speak the gospel "more courageously and fearlessly."** Who in your life has inspired you to be braver in your faith? What was it about their example that made a difference?

Paul has told the Philippians about his situation. The gospel is advancing. He expects to be released. He plans to come back to them. But before he gets there, he has something urgent to say about how they're living right now, especially about standing together when the pressure is on.

Turn the page.

3

STANDING FIRM TOGETHER

"Ducks fly together." If you've seen *The Mighty Ducks*, you know that line. It's more than a team motto. It's the lesson that transforms the whole movie.

At the start of the film, the team is a disaster. Gordon Bombay, a selfish lawyer forced to coach a ragtag pee-wee hockey team as community service, doesn't care about the kids. The kids don't care about each other. They come from different backgrounds, carry different grudges, and play for themselves. They lose. A lot.

But something shifts. Bombay stops coaching to win and starts coaching for the kids. The players stop trying to be individual stars and start playing as one unit. They learn to trust each other on the ice, to pass instead of shoot, to sacrifice a personal highlight for the good of the team. And when they finally face their toughest opponents, it's not talent that makes the difference. It's unity. One team. One spirit. One purpose.

That's a fun movie about hockey. But Paul is writing about something with far higher stakes. The Philippian church is facing real opposition, real pressure, real suffering. And Paul's message to them sounds a lot like "Ducks fly together," except with a deeper foundation and an eternal purpose. He's calling them to stand firm, stand together, and put each other first, because that's the only way to live a life worthy of the gospel.

CITIZENS OF A DIFFERENT KINGDOM

Paul transitions from talking about his own situation to talking about theirs. And his first command is loaded with meaning. "Whatever happens, conduct yourselves in a manner worthy of the gospel of Christ."

Most English translations use the phrase "conduct yourselves," which is fine, but it misses something important. The word Paul chose was a political word. It had to do with how citizens behave in their city. It meant something like "live out your citizenship." For people living in Philippi, a proud Roman colony whose residents had been granted Roman citizenship by Caesar Augustus himself, that word would have landed with force.

Paul is essentially saying, "You are citizens of a kingdom, but it's not Rome. Live like it."

The Philippians knew what it meant to be a Roman citizen. It came with rights: the right to vote, the right to a fair trial, the right to own property. It also came with responsibilities: loyalty to the emperor, participation in civic life, and devotion to Roman values. Roman citizenship was a big deal. People paid fortunes to get it. Others earned it through military service.

But Paul wants the Philippians to understand that they hold an even higher citizenship. They belong to the kingdom of God. And the values of that kingdom are different from

Rome's. Where Rome valued power, status, and self-promotion, the gospel calls for humility, service, and putting others first. Paul will spell this out more directly later in the letter when he writes, "Our citizenship is in heaven" (3:20). But the seed is planted right here. Live as citizens who are worthy of the gospel of Christ, not as citizens who are trying to climb the Roman social ladder.

ONE SPIRIT, ONE PURPOSE

What does citizenship worthy of the gospel look like? Paul gets specific. "Then, whether I come and see you or only hear about you in my absence, I will know that you stand firm in one spirit, contending as one for the faith of the gospel without being frightened in any way by those who oppose you."

Three things jump out here.

First, Paul wants them to stand firm. This is the language of soldiers holding their ground in battle. Don't retreat. Don't waver. Don't give up territory. The Philippians were living in a city soaked in Roman military pride. Many of the original settlers of the colony had been retired soldiers. Paul is borrowing that imagery and redirecting it. Your battle isn't for Rome. It's for the gospel. Hold the line.

Second, they need to do this "in one spirit." Paul isn't talking about simply agreeing on a few things. He's pointing to the Holy Spirit, the one Spirit who lives in every believer and who is the source of their unity. It's the Spirit who binds them together into one body. Their unity isn't something they manufacture through committee meetings and compromise. It's something the Spirit creates when people submit to God together.

Third, they are to contend together "as one" for the faith of the gospel. The word Paul uses here pictures athletes competing side by side, straining together toward the same goal. It's a team sport, not an individual event. The Philippians can't fight this battle alone, and they aren't supposed to. God designed the church to work as a body, not as a collection of loners.

DON'T BE INTIMIDATED

Paul also addresses the elephant in the room: the Philippians are facing serious opposition. "Without being frightened in any way by those who oppose you. This is a sign to them that they will be destroyed, but that you will be saved, and that by God."

We don't know exactly who these opponents were. They were likely people outside the church who were pressuring Christians to conform to Roman religious and social expectations. In a Roman colony, refusing to participate in the worship of the emperor or the local gods was not just frowned upon. It could cost you your livelihood, your social standing, even your safety.

Paul uses a vivid word for "frightened" here. It was sometimes used to describe a horse being spooked, startled into panic by something unexpected. Paul is saying: Don't let them spook you. Don't let the pressure stampede you into abandoning the gospel.

And then he gives them an astonishing theological perspective. He says their steadfastness in the face of opposition is itself a sign that their opponents are heading toward destruction and that the Philippians are heading toward salvation. Standing firm isn't just brave. It's evidence. It proves whose side God is on.

SUFFERING AS A GIFT

Paul goes further. He doesn't just say, "Hang in there." He reframes the entire experience of suffering. "For it has been granted to you on behalf of Christ not only to believe in him, but also to suffer for him, since you are going through the same struggle you saw I had, and now hear that I still have."

Read that carefully. Paul says suffering for Christ has been "granted" to them. That's gift language. The same God who gave them the gift of faith has given them the gift of suffering. That sounds strange to us. We don't usually think of suffering as something to be grateful for.

But Paul isn't saying suffering is fun or easy. He's saying it has meaning. When you suffer for following Jesus, you are sharing in something that connects you to Christ himself and to every believer who has ever stood firm under pressure. Paul connects his own suffering in prison to the Philippians' suffering in their city. Same struggle. Same Lord. Same purpose. They are partners, not just in ministry but in pain. And that shared suffering, grounded in the gospel, is one of the deepest bonds Christians can have.

THE PLEA FOR UNITY

Now Paul turns from the external threat to an internal one. Opposition from the outside is dangerous, but division on the inside can be fatal.

"Therefore, if you have any encouragement from being united with Christ, if any comfort from his love, if any common sharing in the Spirit, if any tenderness and compassion, then make my joy complete by being like-minded, having the same love, being one in spirit and of one mind."

Notice how Paul builds this appeal. He doesn't bark orders. He doesn't pull rank. Instead, he stacks up four realities that the Philippians already know to be true. You have encouragement in Christ, don't you? You've felt comfort from his love, haven't you? You share in the Spirit together, right? You know tenderness and compassion? Then act like it. If all of these things are real, and they are, then the Philippians have every reason and every resource to be unified.

And the way Paul phrases the request is touching. He doesn't say "obey me" or "get it together." He says, "Make my joy complete." He's appealing to their friendship. He's asking them, as people who love him, to give him the one thing that will make his heart overflow: their unity.

What does that unity look like? Paul repeats himself on purpose. Same mind. Same love. One spirit. One purpose. He's piling up these phrases because he wants to make sure nobody misses the point. This isn't optional. This isn't a nice bonus. Unity is essential to the church's mission.

THE ENEMY OF UNITY

If unity is the goal, Paul names the enemies standing in the way. "Do nothing out of selfish ambition or vain conceit, but in humility consider others better than yourselves. Each of you should look not only to your own interests, but also to the interests of others."

Selfish ambition. That's the same word Paul used back in chapter 1 to describe the preachers in Rome who were trying to hurt him. It describes people who are out for themselves, people who treat the church like a competition where the goal is to come out on top. Vain conceit is the attitude that says, "I'm more important than you are." It's an inflated sense of your own value that leaves no room for anyone else.

These two attitudes are poison to a community. They turn brothers and sisters into rivals. They transform a church from a family into a battlefield. And Paul says flatly: do *nothing* from these motives. Not "try to limit" them. Not "be careful about" them. Nothing.

The alternative? Humility. And here's something most people don't know: humility was not considered a virtue in the Roman world. Greeks and Romans associated it with weakness, with the kind of groveling a slave did before a master. It was something to be avoided, not admired.

But Paul, following Jesus, turns that upside down. In the kingdom of God, humility isn't weakness. It's strength under control. It's the posture of a creature before the Creator, fully aware of who God is and who we are. And it shows up in a very practical way: "consider others better than yourselves." This doesn't mean pretending you're worthless. It means making a deliberate choice to put other people's needs ahead of your own. Their concerns matter more than your comfort. Their well-being takes priority over your preferences.

Paul drives the point home in verse 4: "Each of you should look not only to your own interests, but also to the interests of others." Stop staring inward. Start looking outward. Pay attention to the people around you. Ask what they need. And then do something about it.

WHAT THIS MEANS FOR US

First, your Christ-identity outranks every other identity. The Philippians were Roman citizens living in a proud Roman colony. Paul told them their real citizenship was somewhere else. The same applies to us. You might be American, Canadian, British, or anything else. You might identify with a sports team, a political party, or a social group. None of those things are necessarily bad. But none of them come first. If you belong to Christ, that identity shapes everything else, not the other way around.

Second, unity requires effort, not just agreement. Paul doesn't describe unity as something that happens automatically when people believe the same things. He describes it as something you fight for, something that requires deliberately rejecting selfish ambition and deliberately choosing humility. Real unity costs something. It means giving up the right to always get your way. It means laying down your preferences for the sake of the body.

Third, suffering for Christ connects you to something bigger. When you face pushback for your faith, you aren't alone. You're sharing in a struggle that connects you to Paul, to the Philippians, and to believers around the world and across history who have stood firm under pressure. Suffering isn't meaningless. In the hands of God, it becomes evidence of whose kingdom you belong to.

Fourth, humility is the foundation of every healthy relationship. Selfish ambition and vain conceit destroy families, friendships, and churches. Humility builds them. The practice of looking to the interests of others before your own isn't just a nice idea. It's the operating system of the kingdom of God. And it's exactly what Jesus himself modeled, as Paul is about to show.

TALKING POINTS

1. **Paul uses citizenship language to describe the Christian life.** If the gospel were a country and you were its citizen, what "laws" or values would shape the way you live? How would those values be different from what the culture around you prizes?
2. **Paul says the Philippians should not "be frightened in any way" by their opponents.** What kinds of pressure or opposition do Christians face today? What makes it hard to stand firm, and what helps?
3. **Paul calls suffering for Christ a gift that has been "granted" to Christians.** Why do you think he uses gift language for something so painful? How does it change the way you think about hardship to know it has purpose?
4. **Selfish ambition and vain conceit are the two enemies of unity Paul names.** Which one do you think is a bigger temptation for people your age? What does selfish ambition look like in everyday life, at school, in friendships, or on social media?
5. **Paul says to "look not only to your own interests, but also to the interests of others."** What's one practical way you could do that this week? Why do you think it's so natural to focus on ourselves, and what helps us shift our focus outward?

Paul has told the Philippians what to do: stand together, stay humble, and put each other first. But he knows that telling people to be humble isn't enough. They need to see it. So he's about to show them the most stunning example of humility the universe has ever known.

Turn the page.

4

THE MIND OF CHRIST

Baroness Orczy's *The Scarlet Pimpernel* tells the story of Sir Percy Blakeney, one of the wealthiest and most admired men in England. He has everything: money, title, influence, the respect of society. He could live the rest of his life in total comfort and never lift a finger for anyone.

But across the English Channel, during the French Revolution, innocent people are being dragged to the guillotine every day. And Sir Percy has a secret. Behind his public disguise as a lazy, shallow aristocrat who cares only about fashion and parties, he is actually the Scarlet Pimpernel, a daring rescuer who sneaks into Paris again and again to save condemned prisoners from execution. He risks his life, his reputation, and everything he has to serve people who can never repay him.

Nobody suspects him. That's the whole point. The man with the highest status in the room has chosen, voluntarily, to be underestimated, dismissed, even mocked, so that he can accomplish a mission of rescue. His willingness to descend, to set aside the privileges that were rightfully his, is exactly what makes the rescue possible.

Paul is about to tell the Philippians a story that makes Sir Percy's sacrifice look puny and small. It's the story of someone who didn't just set aside wealth and reputation. He set aside the glory of being God. And he didn't do it for a few years of secret missions. He did it permanently, all the way to a criminal's death. This is the story at the heart of the entire Bible, and Paul places it at the center of his letter for a reason.

HAVE THIS MINDSET

Paul has just finished telling the Philippians to be humble, to consider others more important than themselves, to stop chasing selfish ambition. But telling people to be humble is one thing. Showing them what humility actually looks like is another. So Paul does something breathtaking. He points them to Jesus.

"In your relationships with one another, have the same mindset as Christ Jesus."

That's the setup. The word "mindset" has been all over this letter. It's one of Paul's favorite words in Philippians, and it means more than just thinking. It includes your attitudes, your priorities, the way you see the world and respond to it. Paul has been urging the Philippians toward a shared mindset of humility and love. Now he shows them where that mindset comes from. It comes from Christ himself.

What follows is one of the most famous passages in the entire New Testament. Scholars believe it may have been an early Christian hymn, a song the first believers sang about Jesus. Whether Paul wrote it himself or borrowed it from the worship of the early church, he places it here with laser precision. Every line answers the question: What does it look like to put others first?

THE GREAT DESCENT

"Who, being in very nature God, did not consider equality with God something to be used to his own advantage; rather, he made himself nothing by taking the very nature of a servant, being made in human likeness. And being found in appearance as a man, he humbled himself by becoming obedient to death, even death on a cross."

This is one of the most packed sentences in all of Scripture. Let's slow it down.

It starts at the top: "being in very nature God." Before Jesus was born in Bethlehem, before there was a manger or a star or shepherds, he existed in the full reality of who God is. He wasn't a lesser version of God. He wasn't an angel or a powerful spirit. He was, in his very nature, God. He shared completely in everything that makes God, God.

And then the surprise: "he did not consider equality with God something to be used to his own advantage." This is the opposite of what you'd expect. If you had the power and status of being equal with God, wouldn't you hold onto it? Wouldn't you use it? Every human instinct says yes. In fact, that's exactly what went wrong in the Garden of Eden. Adam and Eve reached for equality with God. They grasped for it. Jesus had it, legitimately and fully, and he chose not to exploit it.

Instead, "he made himself nothing by taking the very nature of a servant." The word Paul uses for "servant" is actually the word for "slave," the lowest position in the ancient world. Think about the distance traveled in this sentence. From the nature of God to the nature of a slave. From the highest possible status in the universe to the lowest possible status in human society. That's not a small step down. That's jumping off a cosmic cliff.

And he did it voluntarily. Nobody forced Jesus to become human. Nobody twisted his arm. He chose it. He "made himself nothing." Paul uses a word that connects directly to what he said back in verse 3 about "vain conceit." The word for "vain" literally means "empty." The Philippians were told not to act out of empty glory. Jesus emptied *himself*. The contrast is sharp: don't chase empty glory; follow the one who embraced emptiness for the sake of others.

But the descent doesn't stop at the incarnation. "Being found in appearance as a man, he humbled himself by becoming obedient to death, even death on a cross."

Jesus didn't just become human. He became an obedient human. He submitted to God the Father completely, following the path laid out for him even when that path led to execution. And not just any death. Death on a cross. In the Roman world, crucifixion was the most shameful form of execution imaginable. It was reserved for slaves and criminals. Roman citizens couldn't be crucified; it was considered too degrading. For a first-century reader, "death on a cross" was the most shocking way to end this sentence. God. On a cross.

The entire movement of these verses goes one direction: down. From God to slave. From glory to shame. From heaven to the cross. Every step is a further act of humility, a further letting go of privilege. And every step is motivated by love for people who could never deserve it.

THE GREAT EXALTATION

But the story doesn't end in the grave. "Therefore God exalted him to the highest place and gave him the name that is above every name, that at the name of Jesus every knee should bow, in heaven and on earth and under the earth, and every tongue acknowledge that Jesus Christ is Lord, to the glory of God the Father."

"Therefore." That word is doing enormous work. It means "because of what Jesus did," because he descended and humbled himself and went all the way to the cross. God responded. And God's response was the opposite of the descent: total, absolute exaltation.

God lifted Jesus to the "highest place." There is no higher rung. There is no promotion beyond this one. The one who went lowest has been placed highest. And God gave him "the name that is above every name." In the ancient world, a name wasn't just a label. It represented who you were, your authority, your identity. The name above every name is the name that carries supreme authority over everything that exists.

And Paul tells us what will happen because of that name: "At the name of Jesus every knee should bow, in heaven and on earth and under the earth, and every tongue acknowledge that Jesus Christ is Lord."

This is staggering language. Paul is drawing from the prophet Isaiah, where God himself says, "Before me every knee will bow; by me every tongue will swear" (Isaiah 45:23). In Isaiah, those words belong exclusively to the God of Israel. Paul takes them and applies them to Jesus. He's making a claim so bold it would have stunned his original readers: Jesus shares the very identity and authority of the God of Israel. Every created being, without exception, will one day acknowledge that Jesus Christ is Lord.

For Christians living in a Roman colony where Caesar claimed to be lord, this was a revolutionary statement. There's only one true Lord, and it isn't the emperor.

And the result of it all? "To the glory of God the Father." The Son's humility brings glory to the Father. The exaltation of Jesus is not a competing glory. It's the ultimate revelation of who God has always been: the one whose power is most fully displayed not in domination but in self-giving love.

NOW LIVE LIKE IT

Paul doesn't let this glorious story float in the air like a nice sermon illustration. He brings it crashing down into everyday life.

"Therefore, my dear friends, as you have always obeyed, not only in my presence, but now much more in my absence, continue to work out your salvation with fear and trembling, for it is God who works in you to will and to act in order to fulfill his good purpose."

"Work out your salvation." This doesn't mean "earn your salvation." Paul has already made it clear that God started this work and will finish it (1:6). What it means is: take the salvation God has given you and live it out. Put it into practice. Let it shape how you treat each other. The phrase "with fear and trembling" doesn't mean cowering in terror. It means taking this seriously. The God of the universe has saved you. That should produce awe, not casualness.

And here's the encouragement tucked inside the command: "It is God who works in you to will and to act." You aren't doing this alone. The same God who saved you is actively working inside you, shaping your desires and empowering your actions. God doesn't just tell you to be obedient and then walk away. He moves in and works alongside you.

STARS IN A DARK WORLD

Paul then gets specific about what working out their salvation looks like. "Do everything without grumbling or arguing, so that you may become blameless and pure, children of God without fault in a warped and crooked generation. Then you will shine among them like stars in the sky as you hold firmly to the word of life."

There it is. The grumbling and arguing that were tearing the Philippian church apart, Paul names them directly. These aren't minor issues. When God's people bicker and complain, they look exactly like the world around them. They lose their distinctiveness. They stop shining.

But when the church gets this right, when Christians stop arguing and start living out their salvation with humility and love, something beautiful happens. They shine. Paul borrows language from the book of Daniel, where the faithful people of God are compared to stars (Daniel 12:3). In a world that is "warped and crooked," a united, loving, humble church stands out like a constellation against a dark sky.

And they don't just shine passively. They "hold firmly to the word of life." They hold onto the gospel and hold it out to a world that desperately needs it. The church is both a beacon and a messenger, a community that reflects God's light and offers God's life to everyone around them.

POURED OUT TOGETHER

Paul closes this section with an image that ties his suffering and theirs together. "But even if I am being poured out like a drink offering on the sacrifice and service coming from your faith, I am glad and rejoice with all of you. So you too should be glad and rejoice with me."

A drink offering in the Old Testament was wine poured out at the altar alongside a sacrifice. Paul pictures the Philippians' faithful service as the main sacrifice on the altar, and his own suffering as the wine poured out alongside it. His imprisonment, his hardship, his possible death, all of it is an offering to God, poured out in connection with their faith.

And his response? Joy. "I am glad and rejoice with all of you." Even facing death, even being poured out, Paul rejoices. And he asks them to do the same. "So you too should be glad and rejoice with me." This is mutual joy in mutual sacrifice. It's the picture of a community that has taken the mind of Christ seriously: giving everything, holding nothing back, and finding joy not in comfort but in faithfulness.

WHAT THIS MEANS FOR US

First, true greatness is measured by how far down you're willing to go, not how high you climb. The world says greatness means power, status, and influence. Jesus says greatness means service, sacrifice, and humility. The one who had the highest status in the universe voluntarily descended to the lowest place. If that's the pattern God honors, then every act of humble service you perform, every time you put someone else first, matters more than any trophy or title.

Second, God always lifts up what the world pushes down. Jesus went to the cross, the most shameful death imaginable, and God exalted him above everything. If you're in a season where doing the right thing makes you look weak or foolish, take heart. God's economy works differently from the world's. The humble will be exalted. It may not happen on your timeline, but it will happen.

Third, obedience is powered by God, not just willpower. "Work out your salvation" sounds exhausting until you read the next line: "for it is God who works in you." You aren't doing the Christian life on your own strength. God is working inside you, shaping what you want and empowering what you do. When obedience feels impossible, remember that the God who commands it also supplies the power to carry it out.

Fourth, how you handle conflict says more about your faith than how you handle Sunday morning. Paul doesn't rebuke the Philippians for bad theology. He rebukes them for grumbling and arguing. The way you treat the people around you, especially the ones who frustrate you, is where your faith becomes visible. A church that loves well in the middle of disagreement shines like stars. A church that tears itself apart in bickering disappears into the darkness.

TALKING POINTS

1. **Jesus "did not consider equality with God something to be used to his own advantage."** What privileges or

advantages do you have that you could set aside for the sake of someone else? What makes it hard to let go of things we feel we've earned or deserve?

2. **The Christ hymn traces a downward path: from God to servant, from servant to death, from death to the cross.** Why do you think Paul arranged the story this way? What does this pattern of descent teach us about God's character?

3. **Paul says to "work out your salvation with fear and trembling."** What's the difference between working out your salvation and trying to earn it? How does knowing that "God works in you" change the way you approach the hard parts of following Jesus?

4. **Paul tells the Philippians to stop grumbling and arguing so they can "shine like stars." Think about the groups you belong to: your family, your friend group, your church.** What's one way grumbling or arguing dims the light of that group? What would it look like to shine instead?

5. **Paul describes his suffering as a "drink offering" poured out alongside the Philippians' faith**. What does it mean that he can find joy in being "poured out"? How is that kind of joy different from happiness?

Paul has shown the Philippians the ultimate example of humility. But he's not done with examples. He's about to introduce two real, ordinary men who have lived out the mind of Christ in practical, everyday ways.

Turn the page.

5

FAITHFUL FRIENDS

If you've seen *Homeward Bound: The Incredible Journey*, you know the ending. Shadow, the old golden retriever, has been missing. His two companions made it home, but Shadow didn't appear. Everyone assumes the worst. The boy, Peter, stands at the edge of the yard, staring at the tree line, waiting. And then, limping badly, barely able to walk, Shadow crests the hill. He's hurt. He's exhausted. He nearly died in a mudslide along the way. But he kept going, because getting home to the person he loved mattered more than his own survival.

Peter runs to him. Shadow collapses into his arms. And there isn't a dry eye in the house.

That scene works because it captures something true about loyalty: the people (or animals) who matter most aren't the ones with the flashiest talents. They're the ones who keep showing up, who push through the hard stuff, who refuse to quit even when it costs them everything.

Paul is about to introduce the Philippians to two men like that. Not celebrities. Not miracle workers. Just two faithful servants who have lived out the mind of Christ in unglamorous, everyday, life-risking ways. Their names are Timothy and Epaphroditus. And if the Christ hymn in the previous chapter showed the Philippians what humility looks like in heaven, these two men are about to show them what it looks like on the ground.

TIMOTHY: LIKE NO ONE ELSE

Paul has just finished the most theologically intense section of the letter. He's described Christ's descent from the form of God to the cross. He's told the Philippians to work out their salvation, to stop grumbling, to shine like stars. Now he turns to something more personal: his plans to send Timothy.

"I hope in the Lord Jesus to send Timothy to you soon, so that I also may be cheered when I receive news about you. I have no one else like him, who will show genuine concern for your welfare."

Paul is in prison. He can't visit Philippi himself. So he plans to send the next best thing: Timothy, the person who shares his heart more closely than anyone else on earth.

Notice what Paul says about Timothy: "I have no one else like him." Paul paints a picture of two people whose souls are so aligned that they think and feel the same way. Timothy isn't just obedient to Paul. He actually carries Paul's concerns inside himself. When Paul worries about the Philippians, Timothy worries too. When Paul prays for them, Timothy is right there praying alongside him.

That's rare. And Paul knows it. He immediately contrasts Timothy with unnamed others who have a very different attitude.

"For everyone looks out for their own interests, not those of Jesus Christ."

Sound familiar? It should. Just a few verses earlier, Paul told the Philippians, "Each of you should look not only to your own interests, but also to the interests of others" (2:4). Now he holds up Timothy as someone who actually lives that way. Timothy is the walking, breathing example of the humble mindset Paul has been preaching about.

We don't know exactly who Paul is talking about when he says "everyone" looks out for themselves. He probably doesn't mean literally every Christian in Rome. More likely, he's thinking of people available to send to Philippi, people who could have stepped up but were too focused on their own agendas. Whatever the case, the contrast with Timothy is stark. In a room full of people chasing their own goals, Timothy stands out because he genuinely cares about others.

PROVEN CHARACTER

Paul doesn't stop with his own assessment of Timothy. He reminds the Philippians of what they already know from personal experience. "But you know that Timothy has proved himself, because as a son with his father he has served with me in the work of the gospel."

The Philippians had watched Timothy serve alongside Paul when the church was first planted over a decade earlier. Timothy was there in those early days when Paul and Silas were beaten and thrown in prison (Acts 16). He had seen the hard side of ministry up close and hadn't flinched.

Paul uses a word for "proved himself" that means Timothy had been tested and found genuine, like gold that has been heated in a fire and shown to be real. His character wasn't a theory. It was the result of years of trial, pressure, and faithful endurance.

And the relationship between Timothy and Paul is described in family language: "as a son with his father." Timothy wasn't just Paul's assistant or employee. He was like a son, someone who had absorbed Paul's way of seeing the world, someone who had learned by watching and working beside him day after day, year after year. When Paul couldn't be there in person, Timothy was the closest thing the Philippians could get.

Paul's plan was to send Timothy as soon as his own situation became clearer. If the trial went well, Paul himself would follow: "I am confident in the Lord that I myself will come soon." But in the meantime, Timothy would go first, both to encourage the Philippians and to bring back news that would cheer Paul's heart.

EPAPHRODITUS: THE WOUNDED SOLDIER

While Timothy's visit was still future, there was a more urgent matter. Epaphroditus, the man the Philippians had sent to care for Paul, was going home. And Paul needed to explain why.

"But I think it is necessary to send back to you Epaphroditus, my brother, co-worker and fellow soldier, who is also your messenger, whom you sent to take care of my needs."

Look at the titles Paul piles on this man. Five descriptions in a single sentence. "My brother" means they share a bond as family in Christ. "Co-worker" means they've labored side by side in gospel ministry. "Fellow soldier" is a military image, picturing Epaphroditus as a comrade who has fought alongside Paul in the trenches. Then from the Philippians' perspective: "your messenger" (the word is actually "apostle," meaning someone sent on an official mission) and the one "sent to take care of my needs."

Paul is stacking up honors, and there's a reason. He knows the Philippians might have complicated feelings about Epaphroditus coming home. They had sent him on a mission to serve Paul, but he was returning before that mission was fully complete. Some in the church may have wondered: Did he give up? Was he not strong enough? Why didn't he stay?

Paul addresses that question head-on by telling them exactly what happened.

ALMOST DIED

"For he longs for all of you and is distressed because you heard he was ill. Indeed he was ill, and almost died. But God had mercy on him, and not on him only but also on me, to spare me sorrow upon sorrow."

Epaphroditus had gotten desperately sick, likely during his journey to Rome or shortly after he arrived. We don't know what the illness was, only that it was severe enough to bring him to the brink of death. In a world without hospitals, antibiotics, or emergency rooms, that kind of illness was often a death sentence. People in the first century expected to die from serious disease. Recovery was the exception, not the rule.

Somehow, the Philippians had heard about the illness. Perhaps a traveling companion had carried the news back to Philippi. And now Epaphroditus was distressed, not about his own health, but about *them*. He knew they were worried. He knew they were suffering their own hardships back home. And on top of everything, they were now anxious about whether he was alive or dead.

Paul confirms the worst of their fears: yes, it was that bad. Epaphroditus nearly died. But then Paul points to the only explanation that matters: "God had mercy on him." God intervened. God healed him. And Paul adds, with raw emotion, that God's mercy wasn't just for Epaphroditus. It was also for Paul, "to spare me sorrow upon sorrow." Paul was already carrying the weight of imprisonment. Losing Epaphroditus on top of that would have been devastating.

This is a side of Paul we don't always see. He's not a superhero immune to grief. He's a man who loves deeply and who would have been crushed by the death of his friend. God, in his mercy, spared them both from that heartbreak.

WELCOME HIM HOME

With the crisis over and Epaphroditus recovered, Paul sends him home. But not quietly. He sends him with a command and a commendation.

"Therefore I am all the more eager to send him, so that when you see him again you may be glad and I may have less anxiety. So then, welcome him in the Lord with great joy, and honor people like him, because he almost died for the work of Christ. He risked his life to make up for the help you yourselves could not give me."

Paul is eager to reunite Epaphroditus with his church family. Their gladness at seeing him alive will ease some of Paul's own sorrow. But Paul doesn't just want a polite welcome. He wants a celebration. "Welcome him in the Lord with great joy." Throw a party. Make it clear that this man is a hero.

And then the strongest commendation of all: "Honor people like him, because he almost died for the work of Christ. He risked his life to make up for the help you yourselves could not give me."

The Philippians loved Paul and wanted to serve him, but they were hundreds of miles away. They couldn't visit him in prison. They couldn't bring him food or supplies themselves. So they did the next best thing: they sent Epaphroditus as their representative, carrying their gift and their love. And Epaphroditus took that mission so seriously that he pressed forward even when his body was failing him. He risked his life, not for adventure or glory, but to complete a simple act of service on behalf of his church.

Paul uses language here that echoes the Christ hymn just a few verses earlier. Christ was "obedient to death" (2:8). Epaphroditus came near "to death" for the work of Christ (2:30). The parallel is deliberate. Epaphroditus isn't Christ, but he's following the same pattern: putting the needs of others ahead of his own safety, serving at great personal cost, and trusting God with the outcome.

TWO ORDINARY HEROES

Step back and look at what Paul has done in this passage. He's just finished painting the most exalted portrait of Christ in the entire New Testament, the one who descended from the form of God to a cross. And now, without skipping a beat, he points to two ordinary men and says, "This is what it looks like in real life."

Timothy models the mind of Christ by genuinely caring about others when everyone around him is focused on themselves. He has proven character. He has stayed faithful through years of unglamorous, day-in-day-out service. No miracles. No dramatic visions. Just steady, selfless work.

Epaphroditus models the mind of Christ by risking his life to serve someone else. He carried a gift across dangerous roads, got desperately sick, nearly died, and kept going. His sacrifice wasn't public or celebrated until Paul wrote about it. He wasn't looking for recognition. He was looking out for the interests of others.

These are the kind of people Paul says the church should honor. Not the loudest voices. Not the most impressive résumés. The faithful ones. The ones who show up. The ones who put others first when nobody is watching.

WHAT THIS MEANS FOR US

First, the church needs people like Timothy. Every church needs people who genuinely care about the welfare of others, not because it's their job but because it's who they are. Timothy wasn't serving because he had to. He was serving because the concerns of Christ and his people had become his own concerns. That kind of character isn't born overnight. It's built through years of faithfulness, through proving yourself in small things before anyone trusts you with big ones.

Second, faithfulness in hard circumstances is worth more than talent in easy ones. Epaphroditus didn't have a flashy ministry. He carried money and supplies to a prisoner. That's it. But he did it at the risk of his own life, and Paul calls him a brother, a co-worker, and a fellow soldier. God doesn't measure greatness the way the world does. He measures it by faithfulness, especially when faithfulness is costly.

Third, it's okay to grieve and to need people. Paul admits that losing Epaphroditus would have piled sorrow upon sorrow. He admits that sending Epaphroditus home will ease his own anxiety. Paul isn't ashamed of needing his friends. The Christian life was never meant to be lived alone. We are allowed to be honest about our grief, and we are allowed to lean on the people God puts in our lives.

Fourth, honor the faithful. Paul tells the Philippians to welcome Epaphroditus "with great joy" and to "honor people like him." Our culture tends to celebrate the famous and the powerful. Paul says: celebrate the faithful. Celebrate the people who show up early and stay late. Celebrate the ones who visit the sick, deliver the meals, and serve behind the scenes. Those people are living out the mind of Christ, and they deserve to be recognized.

TALKING POINTS

1. **Paul says Timothy has "no one else like him" because he genuinely cares about others when most people focus on themselves.** What do you think makes someone genuinely care about other people's problems? Is it something you're born with, or something you can develop?

2. **Paul describes Timothy's character as "proven," meaning it was tested over time and shown to be real.** What are some ways a person's character gets tested? How can hard times reveal whether someone's faith and love are genuine?

3. **Epaphroditus risked his life to bring a gift to Paul in prison. It wasn't glamorous work, just delivering money and supplies.** Why do you think Paul honors him so highly for something that might seem simple? What does this say about how God views ordinary acts of service?

4. **Paul admits that losing Epaphroditus would have caused him "sorrow upon sorrow."** Why is it important that Paul, one of the greatest leaders in Christian history, was honest about his grief? How does his example help you think about expressing your own emotions?

5. **Paul tells the Philippians to "honor people like" Epaphroditus.** Who in your life serves faithfully without getting much recognition? What's one way you could honor them this week?

Paul has given the Philippians three examples of the humble, others-first mindset he's been preaching: Christ, Timothy, and Epaphroditus. But not everyone in the world around them is following that pattern. Some are pushing a very different message. And Paul is about to warn the Philippians about that danger with some of the strongest language in any of his letters.

Turn the page.

6

KNOWING CHRIST

Henry David Thoreau was tired of it. In 1845, at the age of twenty-seven, he looked at the world around him and decided that most people were wasting their lives chasing things that didn't matter. Money. Status. Bigger houses. Nicer clothes. Busier schedules. Everyone was running, but nobody seemed to know what they were running toward.

So Thoreau did something drastic. He walked into the woods near Concord, Massachusetts, built a small cabin by the shore of Walden Pond, and simplified his life down to the basics. He wanted to find out what was truly essential and what was just noise. In his book *Walden*, he wrote, "I went to the woods because I wished to live deliberately, to front only the essential facts of life, and see if I could not learn what it had to teach, and not, when I came to die, discover that I had not lived."

Thoreau stripped away what the world valued and went looking for what was real.

Paul does something similar in Philippians 3, but far more radical. He doesn't walk away from wealth or social status. He walks away from the most impressive religious résumé anyone could build. He lists credentials that would have made any Jewish leader green with envy, and then he uses the ugliest word he can find to describe them. Not "less important." Not "second place." Excrement. And he does it for one reason: he found something so much better that everything else lost its value. He found Christ.

REJOICE, AND WATCH OUT

Paul opens this section with a command that, by now, should sound familiar: "Further, my brothers and sisters, rejoice in the Lord!"

This is the sixth time some form of "joy" or "rejoice" has appeared in this short letter. Paul keeps coming back to it because the Philippians need to hear it. They're suffering. They're under pressure. And Paul knows that their greatest source of strength is not gritting their teeth harder but anchoring their joy in the right place. Not in their circumstances. Not in their achievements. In the Lord.

But then the tone shifts. After telling them to rejoice, Paul fires off one of the most intense warnings in any of his letters.

"Watch out for those dogs, those evildoers, those mutilators of the flesh! For it is we who are the circumcision, we who serve God by his Spirit, who boast in Christ Jesus, and who put no confidence in the flesh."

Who are these people? They were almost certainly Jewish Christians who believed that Gentile believers needed to be circumcised and follow the Jewish law in order to be fully part of God's people. They weren't necessarily in Philippi yet, but

Paul had dealt with them in other churches and knew they could show up at any time. He wanted the Philippians ready.

The language Paul uses is scorching. "Dogs" was an insult that Jewish people sometimes used for Gentiles, people they considered unclean. Paul flips it on the Judaizers themselves: by insisting on outward religious rituals as the key to belonging to God, *they* are the unclean ones. "Evildoers" says their work, however religious it looks, is actually working against God's purposes. And "mutilators of the flesh" is a brutal wordplay. The word for circumcision means "to cut around." Paul swaps in a word that means "to cut to pieces," essentially calling their prized ritual nothing more than self-mutilation.

Why so harsh? Because Paul understood what was at stake. If the Philippians believed they needed to add anything to Christ in order to be right with God, they would be walking away from the gospel itself. The sufficiency of Christ was on the line.

Paul counters with a declaration: "It is *we* who are the circumcision." Not the people who cut the flesh, but the people who worship by God's Spirit, who boast in Christ Jesus, and who put no confidence in the flesh. True belonging to God's people isn't marked by a physical ceremony. It's marked by the Spirit's presence and a heart that trusts in Christ alone.

PAUL'S IMPRESSIVE RÉSUMÉ

But Paul doesn't just make theological arguments. He makes it personal. If anyone could have claimed that religious credentials earned them a spot with God, it was Paul. And he wants the Philippians to know it.

"Though I myself have reasons for such confidence. If someone else thinks they have reasons to put confidence in the flesh, I have more."

Then he rolls out the list:

"Circumcised on the eighth day." He wasn't a convert who came to Judaism later in life. He was born into it, marked as part of God's people from the very beginning. "Of the people of Israel." He belonged to the nation God had chosen. He wasn't an outsider trying to get in. He was born on the inside. "Of the tribe of Benjamin." Not just any Israelite, but from one of the most honored tribes, the tribe of Israel's first king, the tribe whose territory held Jerusalem itself. "A Hebrew of Hebrews." His Jewish identity ran deep. He spoke the language. He lived the culture. He didn't just inherit the faith; he breathed it.

Then Paul moves from what he was given to what he earned. "In regard to the law, a Pharisee." The Pharisees were the most devoted students and teachers of God's law. Paul didn't just know the rules. He mastered them. "As for zeal, persecuting the church." This is a chilling line. Paul's dedication to his religion was so fierce that he hunted down the early Christians, believing he was doing God a favor. "As for righteousness based on the law, faultless." When it came to following the rules, Paul had a perfect record. No one could point to a single violation.

Seven items. Four by birth, three by achievement. If salvation could be earned, Paul had more than enough points on the board. His religious résumé was spotless.

THE GREAT REVERSAL

And then comes the word "but."

"But whatever were gains to me I now consider loss for the sake of Christ."

One sentence flips everything. The credentials Paul had spent a lifetime building? Loss. The status he had earned through sweat and sacrifice? Loss. The perfect record he could have presented to God as proof of his devotion? Loss.

Not just "less important." Not "second priority." Loss. Like money stolen from your wallet. Like a trophy that turns out to be made of plastic.

And Paul isn't done.

"What is more, I consider everything a loss because of the surpassing worth of knowing Christ Jesus my Lord, for whose sake I have lost all things. I consider them rubbish, that I may gain Christ."

Paul expands the category. It's not just his religious achievements that are worthless. *Everything* the world counts as valuable fades to nothing next to knowing Christ. And the word he uses for "rubbish" is the most shocking word available to him. It could refer to garbage thrown out into the street for stray dogs to pick through. It could also mean something cruder: human excrement. Either way, Paul is choosing the most offensive word he can think of to describe the thing he used to be most proud of.

Why? Because he found something infinitely better.

"Knowing Christ Jesus my Lord." This isn't head knowledge. It's not being able to pass a quiz about Jesus. In the Bible, "knowing" someone means having a deep, personal, life-changing relationship with them. It's how a parent knows a child, how close friends know each other. Paul is saying that a living relationship with Jesus is worth more than every advantage, every achievement, every credential the world has ever produced.

Notice the words: "Christ Jesus *my* Lord." Paul usually says "our Lord." Here, it's personal. *My* Lord. This isn't abstract theology. This is a man who has been grabbed by the love of Jesus and can't let go.

A DIFFERENT KIND OF RIGHTEOUSNESS

Paul explains what gaining Christ looks like in practice. "And be found in him, not having a righteousness of my own that comes from the law, but that which is through faith in Christ, the righteousness that comes from God on the basis of faith."

Two kinds of righteousness are on the table. The first is "my own righteousness," the kind that comes from following religious rules. Paul had this one nailed. He was faultless, remember? But he calls it worthless. Not because the law is bad, but because human effort, no matter how impressive, can never be enough to stand before a holy God. Your best day still falls short.

The second kind of righteousness is entirely different. It doesn't come from you. It comes from God. And you receive it not by earning it but by trusting in Christ. This is what Paul calls "the righteousness that comes from God on the basis of faith." God declares you right with him, not because of what you've done but because of what Christ has done. That's the trade Paul made. He gave up self-made righteousness and received God-given righteousness. And it wasn't even close.

THE FELLOWSHIP OF SUFFERING AND RESURRECTION

Paul closes this section with some of the most profound words in any of his letters. "I want to know Christ, yes, to know the power of his resurrection and participation in his sufferings, becoming like him in his death, and so, somehow, attaining to the resurrection from the dead."

"I want to know Christ." After everything Paul has already experienced, after decades of ministry, after writing letter after letter about Jesus, he still wants *more*. The relationship isn't finished. It's not a box to check. Knowing Christ is the pursuit of a lifetime.

And what does deeper knowledge of Christ look like? Two things, inseparable from each other.

First, "the power of his resurrection." The same power that raised Jesus from the dead is at work in Christians right now. It's the power that transforms lives, breaks chains, creates new people out of old ones. Paul wants to experience that power, not as a theory, but as daily reality.

Second, "participation in his sufferings." This is the part most of us would prefer to skip. But Paul puts them together on purpose. You can't have resurrection power without the cross. If Jesus reached glory through suffering, his followers walk the same road. When you suffer for doing what's right, when your faith costs you something, when the world pushes back because you follow Christ, you are sharing in the experience of Jesus himself.

"Becoming like him in his death." Paul isn't talking about literal crucifixion. He's talking about a way of living that mirrors the cross: dying to selfishness, dying to the need for control, dying to the desire for the world's approval. It's the same pattern we saw in the Christ hymn. Down before up. Death before resurrection. Cross before crown.

And the goal of it all: "somehow, attaining to the resurrection from the dead." Paul uses the word "somehow" not because he doubts the resurrection but because he knows the path there is unpredictable. He doesn't know exactly what the road ahead looks like. But he knows where it ends: with Christ, raised and transformed, forever.

WHAT THIS MEANS FOR US

First, nothing you add to Christ makes you more acceptable to God. Paul's religious achievements were the best anyone could offer, and he called them something cruder than garbage. If Paul's perfect record couldn't earn a right standing with God, neither can yours. Salvation comes through faith in Christ, not through being good enough, religious enough, or impressive enough. Rest in that.

Second, knowing Christ is the goal of your life, not just the starting point. Paul didn't say, "I knew Christ and now I've moved on to other things." After years of walking with Jesus, his deepest desire was still to know him more. The Christian life isn't a graduation. It's a relationship that deepens over a lifetime.

Third, suffering for Christ isn't an accident. It's part of the package. Paul didn't separate the power of the resurrection from participation in Christ's sufferings. They come together. If your faith never costs you anything, you might be missing something. When following Jesus leads to difficulty, you're not on the wrong road. You're on the same road Jesus walked.

Fourth, your past doesn't define you, whether it's impressive or shameful. Paul had an incredible religious past, and he let it go. Some of us have pasts full of achievements we're tempted to trust in. Others have pasts full of failures we're tempted to be defined by. Either way, Christ changes the equation. Your identity is found in him, not in what you've done or failed to do.

TALKING POINTS

1. **Paul had an extremely impressive religious background, but he called it all "rubbish" compared to knowing Christ.** What are some things people today are tempted to trust in for their standing with God? Why is it hard to let go of the idea that we can earn God's approval?

2. **Paul says there are two kinds of righteousness: one based on your own effort and one that comes from God through faith.** In your own words, what's the difference? Why does Paul say the first kind is worthless even when it's "faultless"?

3. **Paul says he wants to know "the power of his resurrection and participation in his sufferings."** Why do you think he puts those two things together? Can you have one without the other?

4. Paul uses the phrase "Christ Jesus my Lord," making it personal. What's the difference between knowing *about* Jesus and actually knowing him? What does a personal relationship with Jesus look like in everyday life?

5. **Paul was willing to lose everything for the sake of knowing Christ.** Is there anything in your life that would be

hard to give up if following Jesus required it? What helps you hold your plans and achievements loosely?

Paul has told his story: the credentials he abandoned, the Christ he gained, the resurrection he's chasing. But he's not finished running. He hasn't crossed the finish line yet, and he knows it. What does it look like to keep pressing forward when the prize is still ahead of you?

Turn the page.

7

PRESSING TOWARD THE GOAL

Daniel "Rudy" Ruettiger had one dream: to play football at the University of Notre Dame. The problem was that everything was stacked against him. He was too small. His grades weren't good enough. His family thought he was foolish for even trying. He applied to Notre Dame three times and was rejected each time. When he finally got in, he made the practice squad but was told he'd probably never see actual playing time. Two years on the scout team, getting beaten up in practice every day, and never once setting foot on the field during a real game.

But Rudy didn't quit.

The 1993 film *Rudy* tells his story, and the ending is unforgettable. In the final home game of his senior year, Rudy's teammates petition the coach to let him suit up. He gets in for the last play. He sacks the quarterback. The crowd erupts. His teammates carry him off the field on their shoulders.

Twenty-seven seconds of playing time. That's all he got. But those twenty-seven seconds were the culmination of years of relentless effort, stubborn refusal to give up, and single-minded devotion to one goal. Rudy didn't look back at his failures.

He didn't dwell on the rejections. He fixed his eyes on the finish line and ran.

That's exactly the image Paul paints in the next section of Philippians. He hasn't arrived yet. He knows it. But he's not going to stop running. And he wants the Philippians to run with him.

NOT THERE YET

Paul has just told the Philippians about the greatest trade he ever made, swapping his entire religious résumé for the surpassing worth of knowing Christ. He talked about wanting to know the power of Christ's resurrection and to share in his sufferings. It was passionate, soaring language.

But now Paul pauses and makes something clear: he's not claiming to have it all figured out.

"Not that I have already obtained all this, or have already arrived at my goal, but I press on to take hold of that for which Christ Jesus took hold of me."

This is important. Paul, one of the most influential apostles in Christian history, says he hasn't arrived. He hasn't crossed the finish line. He isn't spiritually complete. There's still more to know, more to experience, more to become.

But instead of being discouraged by that, Paul is energized. The fact that the prize is still out ahead of him gives him a reason to keep running. And notice the beautiful picture in the second half of the verse: "I press on to take hold of that for which Christ Jesus took hold of me." Christ grabbed Paul first. On the road to Damascus, Jesus intercepted a man who was running in the wrong direction and turned him around completely. Now Paul's whole life is spent running toward the One who grabbed him. Christ took hold of Paul. Now Paul wants to take hold of Christ.

ONE THING I DO

Paul drives the point deeper with some of the most memorable words in the letter. "Brothers and sisters, I do not consider myself yet to have taken hold of it. But one thing I do: Forgetting what is behind and straining toward what is ahead, I press on toward the goal to win the prize for which God has called me heavenward in Christ Jesus."

"One thing I do." That's the heartbeat of the passage. Not ten things. Not a complicated strategy. One thing. Everything else falls away. The past, the failures, the achievements, the regrets, the religious résumé he just called garbage—all of it gets left behind. Paul isn't interested in looking in the rearview mirror. He's locked in on what's ahead.

The language Paul uses here is vivid. "Straining toward what is ahead" paints a picture of a runner in the final stretch of a race, every muscle taut, body leaning forward, eyes fixed on the finish line. This isn't a casual jog. It's an all-out sprint. And the finish line isn't vague. It's "the prize for which God has called me heavenward in Christ Jesus."

What is the prize? Paul has already told us. It's Christ himself. It's the fullness of knowing him. It's the resurrection from the dead (3:11). It's standing before Christ, complete and transformed, at the end of all things. Everything Paul has described in this letter points to that moment: the day when he finally gains what Christ gained for him.

And Paul wants the Philippians to understand that this prize isn't something he earns by running hard enough. It's something God has *called* him to. The race matters. The effort matters. But the prize is a gift, held out by a God who is inviting his people home.

FOLLOW THIS EXAMPLE

Paul now shifts from telling his story to applying it. "All of us, then, who are mature should take such a view of things. And if on some point you think differently, that too God will make clear to you. Only let us live up to what we have already attained."

"Mature" is a clever word choice here. Paul just said he hasn't "arrived at the goal." But he calls himself and the Philippians "mature." The two aren't contradictions. You can be mature without being finished. Maturity, for Paul, isn't about being perfect. It's about having the right mindset, the right orientation, the right direction. Mature Christians know they haven't arrived. They know the prize is still ahead. And they keep pressing on.

If some of the Philippians see things differently, Paul doesn't panic. He trusts God to bring clarity in time. But in the meantime, one thing is non-negotiable: "Let us live up to what we have already attained." Don't slide backward. Don't lose the ground you've already gained. Keep walking the road you're on.

Then Paul makes the application explicit: "Join together in following my example, brothers and sisters, and just as you have us as a model, keep your eyes on those who live as we do."

Paul isn't being arrogant. He's being practical. Young Christians need models. They need real people, not just abstract principles, who show them what the Christian life looks like in practice. Paul has modeled it: letting go of the past, counting everything as loss for Christ, pressing toward the goal, embracing suffering along the way. Now he says: follow this pattern. And look for others who live the same way.

A WARNING WITH TEARS

But not everyone follows that pattern. And Paul's tone shifts suddenly. "For, as I have often told you before and now tell you again even with tears, many live as enemies of the cross of Christ. Their destiny is destruction, their god is their stomach, and their glory is in their shame. Their mind is set on earthly things."

Paul is weeping as he writes this. These aren't angry tears. They're tears of grief for people who should know better but have chosen a different path. He's told the Philippians about this danger before, and now he raises the alarm again.

Who are these people? Paul's description is strong but somewhat general. They are "enemies of the cross." That doesn't necessarily mean they hate Jesus openly. It may mean they've rejected the way of the cross, the path of self-sacrifice and suffering that Paul has been describing throughout this letter. They want the benefits of knowing Christ without the cost. They want resurrection power without participation in suffering. They want the crown without the cross.

Paul gives four descriptions of them, and each one contrasts with what he's been teaching.

"Their destiny is destruction." While Paul presses toward the prize of eternal life, their road ends in ruin. "Their god is their stomach." While Paul serves Christ as Lord, they serve their own appetites and desires. "Their glory is in their shame." While believers will share in Christ's glory, these people celebrate things that should embarrass them. "Their mind is set on earthly things." While Paul strains toward the heavenly prize, they've planted their feet firmly in the present world and refuse to look up.

This is the opposite of the mindset Paul has been urging throughout the letter. Instead of humility, self-promotion. Instead of the cross, comfort. Instead of heaven, earth. Paul weeps because he knows where that road leads.

CITIZENS OF HEAVEN

From the dark warning, Paul pivots to one of the most glorious statements in the letter. "But our citizenship is in heaven. And we eagerly await a Savior from there, the Lord Jesus Christ, who, by the power that enables him to bring everything under his control, will transform our lowly bodies so that they will be like his glorious body."

Remember back in chapter 1, Paul told the Philippians to live as citizens worthy of the gospel? Now he tells them where their citizenship actually is. Not Rome. Not Philippi. Heaven.

This would have struck the Philippians like a thunderbolt. They lived in a Roman colony, a city that took enormous pride in its connection to Rome. Roman citizenship was one of the most prized possessions in the ancient world. It meant protection. Privilege. Status. And the emperor was called "Lord and Savior," the one who kept the peace and provided for his people.

Paul takes every one of those claims and hands them to Jesus. Our real citizenship is in heaven. Our real Savior isn't Caesar. He is the Lord Jesus Christ. And what will this Savior do? Something no emperor could dream of. He will "transform our lowly bodies so that they will be like his glorious body."

The bodies that get tired. The bodies that get sick. The bodies that suffer and age and eventually die. Christ is going to transform them. The word Paul uses for "lowly" is the same word he used in chapter 2 for Christ's humiliation. Just as Christ went from the form of God to the humblest form of humanity, and God lifted him to the highest place, so Christians will travel the same path. Our current humiliation, including the suffering the Philippians are enduring, is not the end of the story. Transformation is coming.

And the power behind this transformation is staggering: "the power that enables him to bring everything under his control." Everything. Every empire. Every enemy. Every force that has ever opposed God's people. Christ has the power to subject it all. The same power that will one day bring the entire universe under his authority is the power that will transform your body into the likeness of his glory.

For a suffering church in a Roman colony where the emperor claimed to be lord of the world, this is the ultimate encouragement. Your Lord is bigger. Your future is brighter. And the one who holds your destiny holds everything else too.

STAND FIRM

Paul wraps up this long section with one of the warmest verses in the letter. "Therefore, my brothers and sisters, you whom I love and long for, my joy and crown, stand firm in the Lord in this way, dear friends!"

Count the terms of affection: brothers and sisters, loved, longed for, joy, crown, dear friends. Paul piles them up because he wants the Philippians to feel how much he cares before he gives the final command. And the command echoes where we started back in 1:27—*stand firm*.

Stand firm in the Lord. Don't be shaken by opposition from outside. Don't be divided by conflict on the inside. Don't be seduced by people whose minds are set on earthly things. Don't lose sight of the heavenly prize. Plant your feet on Christ and don't move.

The word "crown" is an athletic image, the wreath given to the winner of a race. Paul is saying that the Philippians themselves are his crown. When the race is over and the day of Christ arrives, they will be the evidence that Paul's life and labor mattered. They are the prize he's running for, alongside Christ himself.

WHAT THIS MEANS FOR US

First, spiritual maturity doesn't mean you've arrived. It means you know you haven't. Paul, the great apostle, said he was still pressing on. If he wasn't finished, neither are you. Maturity isn't the absence of struggle. It's the willingness to keep growing, to keep running, to keep reaching for Christ even when the finish line isn't in sight.

Second, the past doesn't get a vote on your future. Paul forgot what was behind. That includes both his failures and his impressive achievements. You are not defined by your worst mistakes. You are not defined by your greatest accomplishments either. What defines you is the direction you're running right now. Eyes forward.

Third, be careful what you set your mind on. The enemies of the cross weren't destroyed by dramatic sins. They were destroyed by misdirected focus: earthly things instead of heavenly ones. The danger for most of us isn't that we'll openly reject Christ. It's that we'll slowly let lesser things steal our attention until we've forgotten where we're supposed to be headed.

Fourth, your future is more real than your present suffering. Paul told a suffering church that their citizenship was in heaven and that Christ would transform their broken bodies into the likeness of his glorious body. Whatever you're going through right now, it is temporary. The transformation Christ has planned for you is permanent. The power that will make it happen is the power that controls the entire universe. Hold on.

TALKING POINTS

1. **Paul says, "One thing I do: forgetting what is behind and straining toward what is ahead."** What are some things from the past, good or bad, that people your age tend to get stuck on? How does Paul's example help you think about letting those things go?

2. **Paul calls himself "mature" even though he says he hasn't arrived at the goal yet.** What does that tell you about what spiritual maturity actually looks like? How is that different from the way most people define maturity?

3. **Paul describes people whose "mind is set on earthly things" as enemies of the cross.** What are some "earthly

things" that compete for your attention and focus today? How can you tell when something good has started to take the place that belongs to Christ?

4. **Paul says "our citizenship is in heaven" and that Jesus, not the Roman emperor, is Lord and Savior.** What does it look like to live as a citizen of heaven while still living in this world? Are there places where loyalty to Christ and loyalty to your culture might conflict?

5. **Paul calls the Philippians his "joy and crown."** Who in your life has invested in your faith the way Paul invested in the Philippians? How could you let them know what their investment has meant to you?

Paul has told the Philippians to stand firm, to keep their eyes on the prize, and to live as citizens of heaven. But he still has some final words of wisdom to share, including practical instructions on joy, peace, and the secret of true contentment.

Turn the page.

8

THE SECRET OF CONTENTMENT

O. Henry's short story "The Gift of the Magi" is about a young married couple, Jim and Della, who are desperately poor. Christmas is coming, and each of them owns exactly one thing of real value. Della has beautiful, long hair that falls below her knees. Jim has a gold pocket watch that belonged to his father.

Each one secretly sells their treasure to buy a gift for the other. Della cuts and sells her hair to buy a platinum chain for Jim's watch. Jim sells his watch to buy a set of jeweled combs for Della's hair. When they exchange gifts on Christmas Eve, they discover what's happened. The combs are useless without the hair. The chain is useless without the watch. From the world's perspective, they've both made a terrible deal.

But O. Henry doesn't see it that way. He calls them the wisest gift-givers of all, because their love was worth more than anything they gave up to express it. The gifts failed. The love didn't.

That story captures something essential about the final chapter of Philippians. Paul is in prison. The Philippians are suffering. And yet what passes between them—a gift of money carried by a man who nearly died delivering it, a letter of gratitude written in chains—is not a transaction. It's love. And Paul wants the Philippians to know that this kind of love, rooted in Christ and expressed through sacrifice, is the most valuable thing in the universe.

TWO WOMEN WHO NEED TO TALK

Paul begins this final section of the letter by naming names. "I plead with Euodia and I plead with Syntyche to be of the same mind in the Lord."

After chapters of building the case for unity, humility, and a shared mindset, Paul finally gets specific. Two women in the Philippian church, Euodia and Syntyche, are at odds with each other. We don't know the details of their disagreement. Paul doesn't tell us, which probably means the Philippians already knew. What we do know is that these women weren't troublemakers or outsiders. They were leaders. Paul calls them co-workers who "contended at my side in the cause of the gospel." They had been there from the beginning, laboring alongside Paul when the church was first planted. They were the real deal.

Which is exactly why the conflict was so dangerous. When leaders disagree, it doesn't stay between them. It ripples through the whole community. Paul had been writing about unity for three chapters. Now we see why.

Notice that Paul doesn't take sides. He pleads with each woman individually, using the same word for both. He asks a trusted companion in Philippi to help them work it out. And then he reminds the whole church that these women, along with Clement and the rest of the co-workers, have their "names written in the book of life." That's not a threat. It's a reminder.

You all belong to God. You're all headed for the same eternal home. Whatever is dividing you now is infinitely smaller than what unites you.

REJOICE. ALWAYS.

With the specific appeal finished, Paul launches into a rapid series of closing instructions that read like a greatest-hits collection of Christian living.

"Rejoice in the Lord always. I will say it again: Rejoice!" This is the command that runs like a river through the entire letter. Paul has said it in a Roman prison, while facing a trial that could end his life, while dealing with people who preached Christ out of spite, while writing to a church under pressure. And he doesn't say it once and move on. He says it twice. "I will say it again: Rejoice!" As if to make sure nobody thinks he's exaggerating. This isn't an accident. It's a lifestyle. Joy in the Lord is the default setting for the Christian, not because life is easy but because the Lord is real.

"Let your gentleness be evident to all. The Lord is near. Do not be anxious about anything, but in every situation, by prayer and petition, with thanksgiving, present your requests to God."

Three instructions stacked on top of each other, each one connected to the one before it.

Be gentle. The word Paul uses carries the idea of being gracious, reasonable, not insisting on your own rights. Let that gentleness be visible to everyone, even the people opposing you. Why? Because "the Lord is near." That brief sentence works on two levels. Christ is near in the sense that he is present with his people right now, close enough to lean on. And he is near in the sense that his return is coming, which puts everything into perspective.

Don't be anxious. Instead, pray. Bring everything to God. Hold nothing back. And do it "with thanksgiving." That last phrase is crucial. Prayer soaked in gratitude changes the atmosphere. It reminds you who God is and what he's already done. It takes your eyes off the problem and fixes them on the One who holds every solution.

And what happens when you pray this way? "And the peace of God, which transcends all understanding, will guard your hearts and your minds in Christ Jesus."

The peace of God is not the absence of problems. It's a sense of wholeness and security that doesn't make logical sense given your circumstances. It "transcends all understanding," meaning it goes beyond what your brain can figure out on its own. You can't think your way to this peace. It comes from God, and it works like a military guard posted around your heart and mind, protecting them from the anxiety that wants to break in.

THINK ON THESE THINGS

Paul then gives the Philippians a list of things to fill their minds with. "Finally, brothers and sisters, whatever is true, whatever is noble, whatever is right, whatever is pure, whatever is lovely, whatever is admirable, if anything is excellent or praiseworthy, think about such things. Whatever you have learned or received or heard from me, or seen in me, put it into practice. And the God of peace will be with you."

This is Paul's filter for what deserves space in your head. True. Noble. Right. Pure. Lovely. Admirable. Excellent.

Praiseworthy. Paul isn't listing abstract philosophical categories. He's giving the Philippians a grid for evaluating what they allow to shape their thinking, especially in a culture that constantly pushed values at odds with the gospel.

And he follows the thinking with doing: "Whatever you have learned or received or heard from me, or seen in me, put it into practice." Paul isn't just telling them to have good thoughts. He's telling them to live the way he taught them to live. And the promise attached to this obedience is stunning: "The God of peace will be with you." Not just the peace of God (verse 7) but the God of peace himself. The source, not just the gift.

THE SECRET PAUL LEARNED

Now Paul turns to the matter that has been waiting in the background since the beginning of the letter: the Philippians' financial gift, carried to him by Epaphroditus.

"I rejoiced greatly in the Lord that at last you renewed your concern for me. Indeed, you were concerned, but you had no opportunity to show it."

Paul is careful. He doesn't want them to think he's ungrateful or that he's hinting for more. He knows their previous silence wasn't lack of love. It was lack of opportunity. And now that the opportunity came, they jumped at it.

But Paul also doesn't want them to think his joy depends on their money. So he shares a secret. "I am not saying this because I am in need, for I have learned to be content whatever the circumstances. I know what it is to be in need, and I know what it is to have plenty. I have learned the secret of being content in any and every situation, whether well fed or hungry, whether living in plenty or in want."

"I have learned." That means contentment didn't come naturally to Paul. Nobody is born content. It's a skill, developed through experience, forged in both abundance and emptiness. Paul has been well fed and he's been starving. He's had plenty and he's had nothing. And through it all, he has learned a secret.

The ancient philosophers talked about contentment too. The Stoics said you could achieve it through sheer willpower, by training yourself not to care about external circumstances. Paul's contentment sounds similar on the surface, but the foundation is completely different.

"I can do all this through him who gives me strength."

That verse, Philippians 4:13, is one of the most famous and most misused verses in the Bible. People put it on bumper stickers and sports jerseys, as if Paul is saying, "I can win any game, ace any test, achieve any dream through Christ." But that's not what Paul is talking about. Read it in context. He's talking about going hungry. He's talking about being locked up. He's talking about losing everything and still being okay. "I can endure all this," he's saying, "because Christ is the one sustaining me." The power isn't for conquering the world. It's for surviving it with your faith intact.

Paul's contentment isn't built on his own toughness. It's built on Christ's sufficiency. When everything else is stripped away, Christ is still there. And Christ is enough.

A GIFT THAT PLEASES GOD

Even though Paul's contentment doesn't depend on their gift, he makes sure the Philippians know their generosity matters.

"Yet it was good of you to share in my troubles. Moreover, as you Philippians know, in the early days of your acquaintance with the gospel, when I set out from Macedonia, not one church shared with me in the matter of giving and receiving, except you only."

No other church did this. Not one. The Philippians were the only congregation that entered into this kind of financial partnership with Paul. They sent him money when he was in Thessalonica. They supported him during his early travels. And now, years later, they've done it again. Paul remembers every bit of it.

But he reframes their gift in a way they probably didn't expect. "I have received full payment and have more than enough. I am amply supplied, now that I have received from Epaphroditus the gifts you sent. They are a fragrant offering, an acceptable sacrifice, pleasing to God."

Paul takes a financial gift and describes it in the language of worship. "A fragrant offering." In the Old Testament, when a sacrifice was properly offered, the smoke rose from the altar and was described as a pleasing aroma to God. Paul is saying that the Philippians' gift, a bag of coins carried across dangerous roads by a man who nearly died, is as beautiful to God as the finest sacrifice ever placed on an altar. Their generosity is worship.

And then comes one of the great promises in Scripture.

"And my God will meet all your needs according to the riches of his glory in Christ Jesus."

The Philippians gave out of their poverty to meet Paul's need. Now Paul assures them that God will meet *all* of their needs. Not some. All. And not out of limited resources, but "according to the riches of his glory in Christ Jesus." The God who owns the universe will provide for the people who gave sacrificially to serve his purposes. It's not a blank check for material wealth. It's a promise that God will supply whatever his people need to live faithfully and fully for him.

Paul can't help himself. The promise pushes him straight into worship: "To our God and Father be glory for ever and ever. Amen."

GREETINGS FROM THE UNLIKELIEST PLACE

Paul closes the letter with a brief set of greetings, and one of them is extraordinary. "Greet all God's people in Christ Jesus. The brothers and sisters who are with me send greetings. All God's people here send you greetings, especially those who belong to Caesar's household."

Caesar's household. The emperor's own staff. Remember chapter 1, where Paul said the palace guard had heard the gospel? Now we learn that some of them, or others connected to the imperial household, have become Christians. The gospel Paul preached from a prison cell has penetrated the heart of the Roman Empire. The people who serve the man who claims to be lord are now confessing that Jesus is Lord.

It's the perfect ending to this letter. The gospel cannot be chained.

"The grace of the Lord Jesus Christ be with your spirit. Amen."

WHAT THIS MEANS FOR US

First, unity requires naming the problem, not ignoring it. Paul didn't tiptoe around the conflict between Euodia and Syntyche. He called them by name, pleaded with them directly, and asked the community to help. When there's a real rift between people in a church, a family, or a friend group, pretending it doesn't exist doesn't make it go away. Sometimes love means stepping into the awkwardness and doing the hard work of reconciliation.

Second, joy is a decision, not a feeling. Paul commands the Philippians to rejoice, and he says it twice to make sure they hear him. That means joy isn't something you wait around for until your circumstances improve. It's something you choose, rooted in who God is, not in how your day is going. You can be honest about pain and still choose joy, because joy and suffering are not opposites in the Christian life.

Third, anxiety has an antidote, and it isn't trying harder. Paul doesn't say, "Stop worrying and pull yourself together." He says, "Pray. Bring everything to God. Do it with thanksgiving." And the result isn't that all your problems vanish. The result is peace, the kind that doesn't make logical sense, the kind that guards your heart like a soldier standing watch. The cure for anxiety isn't more control. It's more trust.

Fourth, contentment comes from Christ, not from circumstances. Paul learned to be content whether he had plenty or nothing, and his secret wasn't willpower. It was Christ. "I can do all this through him who gives me strength" doesn't mean you can *accomplish* anything you dream of. It means you can *endure* anything life throws at you because Christ is sustaining you. When everything else is stripped away, he is still enough.

TALKING POINTS

1. **Paul pleads with Euodia and Syntyche to "be of the same mind in the Lord." He doesn't take sides or tell one of them she's wrong.** What does that approach teach us about how to handle conflict? When two people you care about are at odds, what role can you play in helping them come back together?

2. **Paul says, "Do not be anxious about anything, but in every situation, by prayer and petition, with thanksgiving, present your requests to God."** What's the difference between worrying about something and praying about it? Why do you think Paul adds "with thanksgiving" to the instruction about prayer?

3. **Paul says he has "learned the secret of being content in any and every situation."** What does it mean that contentment is something he *learned*? What circumstances in your own life make contentment hardest? What would it look like to practice contentment this week?

4. **Philippians 4:13 is one of the most quoted and most misunderstood verses in the Bible. In context, Paul is talking about enduring hunger and hardship, not winning games or achieving goals.** How does understanding the real context change the way you hear that verse? What does it actually promise?

5. **Paul says the Philippians' gift to him was "a fragrant offering, an acceptable sacrifice, pleasing to God."** What

does it mean that an act of generosity can be an act of worship? How does knowing that God sees and values your sacrifices change the way you think about giving your time, money, or energy to help someone else?

And that's Philippians.

A letter written from chains that overflows with joy. A plea for unity grounded in the most astonishing act of humility the universe has ever seen. A warning against settling for less than Christ. A promise that the God who started a good work will finish it.

Paul wrote this letter because he loved a church that loved him back, because the gospel was at stake, and because Christ was everything to him. From beginning to end, the letter orbits one central reality: Jesus Christ is Lord. He is the one who descended from heaven to a cross. He is the one God exalted above every name. He is the one whose mind we are called to share, whose sufferings we are invited to enter, whose resurrection we are promised to experience.

And here, at the end, the same truth Paul declared at the start still holds: "He who began a good work in you will carry it on to completion until the day of Christ Jesus." The story isn't over. The God who saved you is still at work. The prize is still ahead. And the Lord who is near will see you through.

The letter is finished. But the life it calls you to is just beginning.

www.ingramcontent.com/pod-product-compliance
Ingram Content Group UK Ltd.
Pitfield, Milton Keynes, MK11 3LW, UK
UKHW020420250726
13967UKWH00007B/2744